GRIZZLIES

AND ◆ BLACK ◆ BEARS

BEAUTIFUL BRITISH COLUMBIA®

Published by
Beautiful British Columbia
A Division of Great Pacific Industries Inc.

President: John L. Thomson
Director of Publishing: Tony Owen
Editor-in-Chief: Bryan McGill
Art Director: Ken Seabrook
Project Editor: Bruce Obee

To order copies of this book call
1-800-663-7611 in Canada or the U.S.
250-384-5456 worldwide.
Fax: 250-384-2812

Beautiful British Columbia
929 Ellery Street
Victoria, B.C.
V9A 7B4

Printed and bound in Vancouver, B.C.
by Quebecor Printing.

Colour separations and film
in Vancouver, B.C.
by WYSIWYG Prepress

Photography by
Victoria Hurst
and
Thomas Kitchin

Text by
Bruce Obee

Design by
Ken Seabrook

ISBN 0-920431-49-6
1. Grizzly bear – British Columbia.
2. Black bear – British Columbia.
3. Grizzly bear – British Columbia –
Pictorial works. 4. Black bear – British
Columbia – Pictorial works. I. Kitchin,
Thomas (Thomas W.) II. Hurst, Victoria
(Victoria N.) III. Beautiful British
Columbia Magazine (Firm) IV. Title.
QL737.C27023 1996   599.74'446
C96-910851-6

**Grizzlies take a
break from fishing
a coastal stream to
reassert their
dominance.**

GRIZZLIES AND BLACK BEARS

British Columbia's largest carnivores face habitat squeeze

It was a particularly big black bear, foraging alone on a patch of fresh spring horsetails in Kootenay National Park. Tom Kitchin was shooting with a long lens from the edge of the meadow. There was a wide space between them, but apparently not wide enough.

"He took exception to me being there," Kitchin recalls. An idyllic scene turned terrible as the bear sniffed an unwelcome scent then bounded toward the photographer at a full gallop. It stopped just short of the camera and stomped aggressively with its heavy forepaws, huffing and woofing angrily. Its message delivered, it returned, momentarily, to the meadow, then suddenly swung round and took another run at the intruder. Standing his full height and shouting, Kitchin hoisted his tripod over his head, then spiked it into the ground, startling the bear into a short-lived retreat.

"He bluff-charged me eight times," recounts Kitchin. "He forced me out of the field, back to the road and right up to my car door. Several hundred feet." Dominance established,

above: **A Rocky Mountain black bear gobbles the last of the autumn wildflowers in preparation for winter hibernation.**

opposite: **Black bears are second only to grizzlies as North America's largest land predators, weighing up to 300 kilograms where food is plentiful.**

previous pages: *Ursus americanus* — the black bear — is the most plentiful of the world's eight bear species. There could be 160,000 in B.C. alone.

above: **A female grizzly lies back in soft grass to suckle her offspring. Mother's milk may supplement a cub's diet for as long as three years.**

opposite: **A brown or grizzly bear shakes water from its massive head as it fishes for chum salmon.**

the bear reclaimed his meadow and left Kitchin trembling in the car.

When he reluctantly stepped out to tidy his camera gear, the bear heard the door open and sprinted back up the road. "He wanted me gone."

It was a lesson for Kitchin, one of Canada's most prolific wildlife photographers. He'd overstepped his ground and survived to achieve a new level of humility. "Now I'm always on my best behaviour around bears," he admits. "There's no such thing as an old, dumb bear photographer."

Over the years Kitchin and Victoria Hurst, his wife and photography partner, have grown sensitive to the plight of North American bears. These animals are losing ground to humans, and now Kitchin and Hurst often pass up good pictures for fear of bothering the bears. "They deserve a certain peace and privacy in their remaining territory," Kitchin muses. "They have so little left to call their own; they don't need us trespassing."

Kitchin's sentiments are shared by British Columbia wildlife experts. Despite an outcry from hunters and other backwoods travellers, access to critical bear ranges may soon be

left: **As strong swimmers, black bears have no hesitation plunging into a swiftly flowing river. Like humans, they often escape summer heat by lying in cool lakes and creeks.**

above: **A keen sense of smell is often a black bear's best tool in detecting intruders. Photographer Tom Kitchin was bluff-charged eight times** **by a black bear in Kootenay National Park.**

limited. People in the woods, however, are not the more serious concern. It's urbanization encroaching on the woods as well as our packing the woods off to sawmills, causing a loss of food, denning sites, and many other elements of nature vital to a bear's survival.

Though British Columbia is one of the grizzly's few remaining strongholds, there are nonetheless concerns about how long it will remain so. Black bears are more adaptable and numerous, but they too face a future of growing cities and dwindling habitat. Within the next half century — eight or 10 bear generations — the human population of British Columbia could double.

People will outnumber bears by at least 60 to 1. Cities and industries will invariably sprawl into traditional wildlife ranges, upsetting migrations and fragmenting the remaining tracts of unbroken habitat.

Some believe that bears, and all large carnivores, are already doomed. Others contend they'll survive if we consider their needs while rearranging the landscape. There is no question, however, that the move to save the bears is gathering momentum and stature.

This newfound affection for wild bears is an about-face from the attitude of our Canadian forefathers. In 1793 the Parliament of Upper Canada passed *An Act to Encourage the*

13

previous pages: **Alaska's Kodiak bears are among the largest of all grizzlies, sometimes weighing more than 400 kilograms.**

above: **Black bears wrestle for positions along the bank of a chum-salmon stream in coastal British Columbia.**

opposite: **By early autumn, a Rocky Mountain black bear is fully fattened for its long winter fast. It may weigh one-third less when it awakens from hibernation in spring.**

Destruction of Wolves and Bears. It was a licence to rid the land of creatures that pioneering settlers feared most and understood least.

Perhaps their fears were an ancestral hangover from earlier European cultures. Old World mythology often cast the bear in an unfavourable light, portraying it as a symbol of evil, anger, greed, voracity, and violence. A Scandinavian fable tells of an heroic Norseman who ate the heart of a bear and drank its blood to gain strength and courage. Chaucer's 15th century *Canterbury Tales* depict the bear as a glutton, shunned for its slovenly habits.

These thoughts were a contrast to the beliefs of some North American natives, who viewed the bear with reverence. Bears continue to represent the supernatural origins of certain aboriginal clans in British Columbia.

The earliest North Americans, who lived much like other wild species, were inhibited by the abundance of large carnivores. Changes in climate and vegetation about 13,000 years ago prompted a decline in prey taken by these big meat-eaters. Archaeologists confirm that the number of fire pits gradually increased as predators declined with their prey species.

Only a few centuries back, California natives were forced by grizzlies to abandon some of their richest lands. They lauded the great bear's demise at the hands of musket-toting Spaniards. All of the state's grizzlies — 10,000 or so — were gone by the early 1920s, yet California still carries a grizzly emblem on its flag.

At one time more than 100,000, perhaps 200,000 grizzlies wandered western North America from northern Mexico to the Arctic. About 55,000 are left, nearly half of them in Canada. There may be as many as 13,000, or as few as 5,000, in British Columbia. Black bears have fared better: there could be half a million across the continent, 120,000 or more in British Columbia.

Through new conservation strategies, British Columbians are attempting to ensure that grizzlies and black bears will always be here. Tougher hunting laws, higher poaching penalties, and more progressive habitat-protection methods have come into being in the 1990s. Entire old-growth watersheds have been preserved, including the Khutzeymateen on British Columbia's northwest coast, Canada's first grizzly-bear sanctuary.

It's early to predict the outcome of these new moves. But the urgency now has been acknowledged: the campaign to save the bears is well under way.

THE GRIZZLY BEAR

Horribilis is a well-earned title

Anyone who's watched a hungry grizzly demolish a ground squirrel's den has seen the bear's legendary strength and tenacity in action. In a hail of grass and dirt, the burrow is torn apart, rodents are unceremoniously scooped from their underground chambers and hastily devoured.

With finger-length claws and paws the size of baseball gloves, the grizzly is a born digger. Its chunky forearms are powered by a mass of muscle that sits on its shoulders in a conspicuous hump. It is undoubtedly the strongest of North American land predators, and unlike the faster wolf or cougar, the bear's brute force and persistence are its most useful traits.

Despite the grizzly's infamous ferocity, the term "carnivore" is perhaps a misnomer for *Ursus arctos horribilis.* Though it occasionally ambushes a moose or caribou, it is too bulky to thrive on big game. It can reach 50 kilometres an hour in a spurt, but compared to predators that regularly chase their prey, the grizzly is sluggish. While its skull shape and some of its teeth fit the carnivore mold, warm-blooded flesh may comprise only 5 or 10 percent of its diet. The modern-day grizzly is really an omnivore, with piglike teeth and rooting habits.

With only humans to fear, the grizzly is confident feeding on open plains and meadows, often a long run from protective forest cover. A

threatened grizzly will stand its ground, when a smaller, more vulnerable black bear would head for the trees.

The habits of both grizzlies and black bears are tied to the types of terrain in which they live. As strong diggers, grizzlies commony feed on

opposite: **A grizzly bear feeds on autumn blueberries. Berries are particularly important to Interior bears before winter hibernation.**

above: **A young grizzly gallops across a Rocky Mountain meadow.**

roots, bulbs, corms, and tubers. With jaws and teeth adapted to crush and grind, they are heavier chewers than black bears, which eat more green vegetation and forest berries. Grizzlies and black bears often wander overlapping ranges, but not without conflict: black-bear cubs and mothers are sometimes prey for grizzlies.

The survival of all bears hinges almost entirely on the amount and quality of nutrition their habitat can provide. A poorly fed female may be unable to produce offspring. For many bears, if a berry crop or other food source fails, sometimes the only option is a nearby garbage dump or campground. There's not much future in that: only a quarter of British Columbia's "nuisance" grizzlies and

black bears are relocated each year; an average of 855 are shot.

Nourishing a body the size of a muskox requires a huge and productive range. A 300-kilogram grizzly may wander 50 to 2,500 square kilometres or more.

Hibernation is a bear's way of curbing its appetite when its favourite foods are buried in snow. In mild, coastal climates, some bears may hibernate only six or eight weeks. In colder areas, a bear may crawl into its den in October and remain there until May. Mothers bearing young in their dens, usually in January or February, hibernate longer than males or females without cubs.

Although their heartbeats and metabolic rates drop during

opposite and above: **While Interior grizzlies rely on berries for winter fat, coastal bears look for salmon as a prime fattener. Some bears fast through six-month hibernations, surviving on stored fat. Here, north-coast bears take advantage of a chum-salmon run.**

left: **A grizzly cub relaxes in a Rocky Mountain dandelion patch.**

right: **A grizzly mother and cubs stand upright for a better whiff of their surroundings.**

hibernation, compared to smaller deep-sleeping mammals like marmots or ground squirrels, bears are light hibernators. They're known to wake up in winter, and occasionally take short walks outside their dens.

The cost of fasting through winter, however, is substantial: a bear comes out of hibernation in spring weighing about one-third less than it did in the fall. In two or three seasons it must eat a year's supply of food to regain all that weight before winter.

Each season brings a particular bounty and every one is vital. Roots, sedges, and the winter-weakened calves of moose, elk, deer, or caribou are among the first meals after hibernation. As fresh vegetation appears, grizzlies follow the receding snow up avalanche chutes, eating horsetails, fern fiddleheads, rushes, grass, and other greenery. Bears roaming between summer berry patches may stop to shred the odd wasp nest or ant hill. While Interior bears concentrate on berries, coastal grizzlies rely on salmon as a prime fat-layering food source before winter. From midsummer to late fall they follow the runs into spawning pools and side channels, vying with eagles, gulls, ravens, and black bears for space along the riverbanks.

Food alone, however, is not the only necessity of life for a grizzly. Although it often feeds in the open, like the black bear, it finds denning sites and shelter in the forest. If bedding areas next to streams or avalanche chutes are logged, a grizzly has nowhere to rest. It may abandon a source of good food. If sheltered denning sites are cleared, there may be no place to hibernate. Using extra energy to stay warm through the cold season could deplete the bear's fat reserves long before spring.

Logging and other backwoods industries bring roads, opening new territory to hunters and poachers. People are the greatest cause of grizzly mortality. Licensed trophy hunters kill an average of 305 a year in British Columbia. Some 2,000 grizzly tags are sold annually, about half to non-residents who may pay well over $10,000 for a guided grizzly hunt. It's estimated that sportsmen spend nearly $3 million a year to hunt British Columbia's biggest bear.

previous pages:
With finger-length claws, a grizzly rips at a salmon while beating the summer heat.

above: **Fights frequently break out between bears in feeding areas. Few are fatal, but the most aggressive bears invariably claim the best fishing holes.**

The "unreported kill" is anybody's guess. Government sources say it's 25 percent of the known kill. Others believe that for every bear taken lawfully there's at least one, maybe two, killed by poachers or vandals.

Overall population estimates vary just as widely. Provincial biologists insist there are 10,000 to 13,000 grizzlies across the province. Private researchers say 5,000 to 6,000 is more realistic.

The World Wildlife Fund suggests the annual grizzly kill — both legal and illegal — should be no more than 3 percent of the population. The Western Canada Wilderness Committee, which opposes the "immoral and unjustified killing of bears in British Columbia," says 11 percent of the province's grizzlies were killed in 1995. In 1996, when a lottery system for grizzly hunting licences was introduced, the province adopted guidelines allowing 4 percent. But the question remains — 4 percent of what total?

What is known is that of all our big carnivores, grizzlies are the slowest

to reproduce. From the age of five or six, a female may raise a couple of cubs every third or fourth year, perhaps a dozen or fewer over a lifetime. Starvation, accidents, predation, and shootings may claim a third, even half the cubs, leaving comparatively few females to carry on the cycle.

Many conservationists would like to see the existing ban on shooting female bears with young extended to all bears. Anti-hunting sentiment is building in urban British Columbia, but in outlying areas hunting is still very much a way of life. With grizzly

numbers declining, however, influential organizations such as the World Wildlife Fund suggest that "the ethical and biological case for killing grizzly bears for sport or trophy hunting is becoming increasingly difficult to make."

Hunting is one cause of grizzly mortality, but the most serious long-term threat is loss of habitat. Industry and urbanization have already extirpated grizzlies from the south coast, the Okanagan, central Chilcotin, and the extreme northeast corner of British Columbia. They're on the brink of extinction across the southern Interior, where COSEWIC — the Committee on the Status of Endangered Wildlife in Canada — recommends grizzlies be classed as "threatened," one step away from officially "endangered."

The consensus among most wildlife authorities is that habitat protection is the best hope for the North American grizzly. British Columbia has already begun. Canada's first grizzly sanctuary was established in 1992 on the north coast at Khutzeymateen. Tatshenshini — prime bear territory in the province's northwest corner — was set aside a year later. Kitlope, the continent's largest intact coastal rainforest, was protected in 1994. Other areas were preserved in the mountains of southeastern British Columbia and elsewhere throughout the province. Groups like the Raincoast Conservation Society continue to push for protection of more unlogged watersheds inhabited by grizzlies.

above: **A female and cubs feed amid spring dandelions in the Rocky Mountains. Spring vegetation is particularly important to bears coming out of hibernation.**

following pages: **A grizzly cub practises climbing on a summer day in the Rockies.**

Preserving large tracts of wilderness is only a partial solution. Grizzlies are wanderers. Travel routes that link their seasonal foraging grounds are as crucial as the feeding areas themselves. As adolescents disperse, or old-timers are forced by food failures into new areas, the need for contiguous ranges becomes more critical. A patchwork of isolated home ranges fragmented by clearcuts, roads, and communities won't work.

"Only by preserving the viability of its habitat can we ensure a future for the grizzly," states British Columbia's Grizzly Bear Conservation Strategy. "The grizzly bear is perhaps the greatest symbol of wilderness. Its survival will be the greatest testimony to our environmental commitment."

Conservationists, hunters, anti-hunters, foresters, and government wildlife managers hold a common interest in the grizzly's future. Even the National Basketball Association's Vancouver Grizzlies team has become a major partner in British Columbia's conservation strategy, supporting a Grizz Ed program for students.

Opinions from all sides differ. But most everyone agrees the special needs of our "greatest symbol of wilderness" cannot be overlooked much longer. It may already be a case of how many for how long. ❧

opposite: **An itchy grizzly rubs its coarse grizzled fur against a well-worn tree. The hair and scent left on the tree may be signals to other bears travelling the same trails.**

following pages: **A sockeye salmon leaps unwittingly into the jaws of a hungry grizzly bear.**

GRIZZLY BEAR
Ursus arctos horribilis

AVERAGE LENGTH:
2.5 metres.

AVERAGE WEIGHT:
Male, 135 to 450 kilograms; female, 95 to 300 kilograms.

LONGEVITY:
20 or 25 years in the wild.

BREEDING AGE
Male, 8 to 10 years; female 5 to 7 years.

LITTER SIZE:
1 to 4, commonly 2.

DIET:
Roots, bulbs, corms, tubers, berries; fawns, calves, ground squirrels, salmon, insects, and occasionally black bears.

PREDATORS:
Humans, other grizzlies.

AVERAGE ANNUAL KILLS AND RELOCATIONS:
Hunters, 305; conservation officers, 55; relocations, 50.

**ATTACKS ON HUMANS IN BRITISH COLUMBIA
(1978 TO 1995):**
4 killed; 30 injured.

CHARACTERISTICS:
Largest North American land carnivore, considered one of the most dangerous predators.

STATUS IN BRITISH COLUMBIA:
A blue-listed "Species at Risk," classified as "Sensitive/Vulnerable"; threatened by habitat loss; population estimates, 5,000 to 13,000.

THE BLACK BEAR

Our second-largest carnivore sleeps in trees

When grizzlies migrated across the Bering land bridge to North America, about 30,000 years ago, black bears took to the trees. Smaller and more agile than grizzlies, they relied on their climbing skills to survive.

above: **Black bears come in many colours, from black to brown, blonde, cinnamon, auburn, smoky grey, or white. Here a** **brown-phase black-bear cub hides in a coastal rainforest.**

opposite: **A full-grown black bear sniffs around for signs of food or trespassers.**

By nature, the grizzly is the more aggressive of British Columbia's two bear species. It evolved as an animal of the tundra, in a treeless terrain with nowhere to hide from enemies. The grizzly is a fighter.

The American black bear, which had ranged across most of North America for three or four million years, undoubtedly foraged in the open until its rival appeared. It was forced into the woods, but through its long evolution never entirely lost its open-ground instincts. If grizzlies today vanish from a part of the tundra, black bears, over a number of generations, may leave the forest to fill the niche.

Ursus americanus is the most abundant of the world's eight bear species. Half to two-thirds the size of a grizzly, the black bear needs less food and can adapt to a greater variety of habitats. From the deserts of Mexico and Arizona, through the rainforests of coastal British Columbia, to the boreal woodlands of the Northwest Territories, the black bear is the only big predator most people ever see.

It is also the one most often involved in human attacks, not because of an aggressive character, but simply because it is more plentiful. Between 1978 and 1995, black bears in British Columbia killed nine people and injured 79; grizzlies killed four and injured 30. Although there were over twice as many black-bear attacks, when you consider that they probably outnumber grizzlies 10 to 1, they were actually involved in comparatively fewer confrontations.

A black bear generally regards *Homo sapiens* as a species to avoid, but it might take human prey when other food is scarce. It is more likely to attack in defence of its young or feeding territory. The grizzly, on the other hand, was given the name *horribilis* because it finds people as tasty as ground squirrels.

So while grizzlies acquired a pugnacious personality, black bears, though by no means docile, learned to retreat. Even on Vancouver Island, where there are no grizzlies, black bears, especially females, rarely forage far from the edge of the woods. In the forests of British Columbia, they spend a surprising amount of time sleeping in treetops, beyond reach of grizzlies, wolves, and other animals that can't climb. Cubs may climb up 40 or 50 metres, then out onto limbs that barely support their weight. Mothers commonly suckle their young in trees.

British Columbia is mainly forests, and while grizzlies prefer to feed in the open, like black bears they find food, shelter, and travel routes in the woods. Both species migrate through the seasons along old, well-worn paths.

above: **A hungry black bear cleans the berries from a mountain ash tree in preparation for a winter without food. Females that give birth to cubs during hibernation may fast for six months while feeding fetuses and offspring.**

opposite: **A fence is no obstacle to a black bear on the move.**

Like mileposts along a route, certain trees are marked by passing bears. Claw and bite marks, usually facing a trail or open area, appear a metre or two above the ground, embellished by fur, mud, and sap. No one knows why bears leave such noticeable signs. They're probably not territory markers, because they appear throughout a range, rather than around its perimeter. It's possible the odours on the trees warn other animals of a bear's movements, reducing potential conflicts. Another theory is that they help bears orient themselves when migrating through places they rarely visit.

Whether bears need route markers is questionable. They appear to have remarkable memories for important places. In one area, cubs that followed a mother to an oak grove returned as adults five years later to feed on acorns. So-called "nuisance bears" have been tranquillized and moved nearly 300 kilometres, only to return a few days later.

There's some speculation that a bear can sense the Earth's magnetic field and find its way with the help of a built-in biological compass. When a berry crop failed in its home range, one radio-collared research bear wandered 200 kilometres from its usual foraging area, taking a rather roundabout route through unfamiliar territory. Its return route was more direct, suggesting it knew where it was and where it was going. While heading back toward its normal feeding grounds, but still far from home, it moved only during the nights, careful not to arouse sleeping bears and people. Celestial navigation did not come into play, as the bear travelled on both cloudy and clear nights. As it approached its own home range, it began travelling on roads and trails in daylight. It went straight into its winter den to hibernate.

Travel routes are reliable places to locate bears. Researchers studying the effects of logging on coastal bear habitat set up cameras along abandoned roads and animal trails in Vancouver Island's Nimpkish Valley. More than half the Nimpkish has been logged since the early 1900s and some replanted forests there are now 70 years old. Canadian Forest Products, the company logging the valley, provided much of the funding for a study that ran from 1992 to 1995.

continued on page 44

THE KERMODE
Spirit bear of the north coast

RON THIELE

The natives of British Columbia's north coast say there's a ghost in the rainforest, a white bear with power to take human form. Some call it the "spirit" or "snow" bear, claiming it wanders the woods fighting evil and rescuing people in distress.

To scientists, this is *Ursus americanus kermodei*, British Columbia's white black bear. It was named in the early 1900s in honour of Francis Kermode, a zoologist with the British Columbia Provincial Museum at the time.

The term "black bear" is the name of a species, and though many are actually black, they also come in shades of brown, blonde, cinnamon, auburn, smoky grey, and white. A white Kermode is a black bear that may have parents and siblings of varying colours.

Once mistaken for misplaced polar bears, white Kermodes have been spotted as far inland as Liard River Hotsprings. But they live mainly in a limited range bounded roughly by the communities of Stewart, Prince Rupert, Hazelton, Terrace, and Kitimat. They seem most plentiful along the shores of Douglas Channel and on Gribbell and Princess Royal islands, south of Kitimat.

The city of Terrace has adopted the Kermode as its emblem, using its likeness on the official flag, stationery, T-shirts, and souvenirs. "Hank," a local Kermode who met an untimely end on a highway, now stands, stuffed and silent, in the municipal council chambers.

Hunting of white Kermodes is banned, but because Kermodes of other colours can produce white offspring, there's a case for protection of all black bears within the white Kermode's known range.

Conservationists now are calling for creation of Spirit Bear Park, an area of pristine rainforests centred around Princess Royal Island, where about one-tenth of the bears are white. "It seems ironic that the white bears are protected from hunting," the conservationists note, "but the habitat that supports their survival is in no way protected from logging."

BEAUTIFUL BRITISH COLUMBIA MAGAZINE

Special Editions *for BC Nature Lovers*

*BIG Pictures
Spectacular
Photography*

*Informative
Educational
Reading*

Our New PARKS Volumes I, II and III

Our New PARKS feature B.C.'s new provincial parks that were created to preserve their wild, pristine beauty forever. Each volume is filled with the awe-inspiring scenery that makes us proud of B.C. Use these SPECIAL EDITIONS to plan your next vacation or weekend getaway to some of the most beautiful wilderness on the Pacific coast. Share the beauty of these newly protected parks with your friends and relations. They make wonderful gifts.

COLLECT THE WHOLE SERIES

Start your collection of Beautiful British Columbia Magazine's SPECIAL EDITIONS. Each one is a stunning 52-page, colourful portfolio of big, beautiful photography combined with great outdoor writing by B.C.'s best wilderness photographers and journalists.

WOLVES, Coyotes and Foxes

Of all B.C.'s predators, it is invariably wolves, coyotes, and foxes – the wild dogs – that arouse the worst and best of the human spirit.

WILDCATS Cougars, Bobcats, and Lynx

These elusive felines have evolved to become the most proficient of all wild hunters. They rely on their formidable weaponry and acute senses to successfully track and hunt down their prey.

ANSWER THE CALL OF THE WILD

Order your SPECIAL EDITIONS from Beautiful British Columbia Magazine today. Order for yourself and for your friends and relations. They are published for B.C. nature lovers like yourself who have heard the call of the wild and want to discover more of B.C.'s parks, wilderness, and wildlife.

SATISFACTION GUARANTEED

Take 30 days to examine your SPECIAL EDITIONS. If you are not delighted, you may return your special editions and receive a full and prompt refund.

ORDER FORM

Yes. Send me the SPECIAL EDITIONS I have selected below:

▶ ORDERED BY:

My Name

Address

City   Prov/State

Country   Postal/Zip Code

Day Phone   Evenings

▶ MAIL THIS SPECIAL EDITIONS ORDER FORM TO:
Beautiful British Columbia, 929 Ellery Street
Victoria, B.C. Canada V9A 7B4.
Fax 1-800-308-4533. Phone 1-800-663-7611.
E-Mail: orders@bbcmag.bc.ca

▶ PLEASE RUSH ME:

PLEASE RUSH ME:		QTY	PRICE EACH	TOTAL
Our New PARKS Volume I	45787M		$6.95	
Our New PARKS Volume II	45795M		$6.95	
Our New PARKS Volume III	45810M		$6.95	
WOLVES, Coyotes, Foxes	45809M		$6.95	
WILDCATS	45790M		$6.95	
GRIZZLIES	61821M		$9.95	

Shipping & Handling	CANADA	USA	OVERSEAS
Up to $30.00	$ 4.50	$ 9.00	$12.00
$30.01 - $50.00	$ 6.00	$10.00	$15.00
$50.01 - $100.00	$ 8.00	$12.00	$20.00
$100.01 - $200.00	$11.00	$18.00	$27.00
$200.01 & Up	$16.50	$27.50	$37.50

SPECIAL EDITIONS Total	
Add 7% GST	
Shipping & Handling –see chart opposite	
Total Amount Enclosed	

▶ ☐ Cheque or Money Order Enclosed. ☐ VISA ☐ MasterCard ☐ American Express

Card No.   Expiry

SESP97

RON THIELE

above:
Conservationists are pressing for a Kermode sanctuary centered around Princess Royal Island, off British Columbia's north coast. One in 10 black bears here are white.

above: **A hungry black bear enjoys an easy meal of peanut butter and watermelon from an upturned garbage can. Black bears, which live near communities throughout British Columbia, occasionally break into houses to steal food.**

Cameras throughout a 73-square-kilometre area were mounted in trees and triggered by infrared sensors. They clicked off more than 4,500 pictures, including 585 of bears. Thirty-four bears were also captured and 26 were fitted with radio collars then telemetrically tracked by ground and air.

One of the most significant discoveries was the bears' reliance on old-growth timber for denning. Even though some hibernated in stands of second-growth, their dens — without exception — were in old-growth structures within those forests. Some bears would choose the largest tree in a grove. A few bears built big, birdlike nests of ferns and mosses in fallen logs, dead trees, or hollow stumps — 68 dens in all.

A den must provide warmth, dryness, and protection from predators such as wolves or cougars. A mother with newborns has neither time nor energy for outside distractions. A few females in the Nimpkish had dens in old cedars, some with entrances 16 metres off the ground. This kind of protection is one advantage a nimble black bear has over a grizzly, which is a poor climber.

A mother bear will have been fasting for weeks, even months, before the birth of cubs in mid-hibernation. Yet even in winter dormancy her metabolic rate must be high enough to feed her offspring, both inside and outside the womb. Her sleep is easily aroused by noises outside the den. A disturbance that takes her from her cubs could be fatal for all.

The fetal development and growth of newborns that goes on in a bear den is extraordinary in the realm of

Outside the den, cubs learn to forage while continuing to feed on mother's milk for up to two years. Researchers in the Nimpkish Valley found cub mortality to be as high as 65 percent. Mortality generally was high: shortly after the study's end, 19 of the 34 bears captured and released by researchers were dead. Others in the area were known to have died. One

below: **Its ears erect, an alert black bear casts a disapproving stare toward a hiker in the outback. Over the past 17 years, there have been nine human deaths and 79 injuries caused by black bears.**

mammalian child rearing. A bear is the only mammal to give birth during hibernation, a time when fat reserves are her sole sustenance. Embryos are produced only if a bear has enough fat to sustain cubs. A female may mate in June, but through a unique process called delayed implantation, the fertilized egg may not implant to the wall of the uterus until late November or early December. Unable to maintain her own metabolism as well as that of her unborn offspring through a long pregnancy, a female bear gives birth to premature cubs. In proportion to their mother, squirrel-sized newborn black bears — 300 or 400 grams — are about one-tenth the weight of many other mammals at birth. Feeding on fat-rich breast milk, they leave the den at three or four months old, weighing about three or four kilograms — 10 times their birth weight.

was found with its most marketable vital organs missing; a radio-collared female was shot and abandoned in a clearcut. Some were hit by trucks, the majority were legally shot by hunters. Surprisingly, and inexplicably, seven bears — four of them cubs — were eaten by other bears: it was the highest rate of cannibalism ever recorded in North America.

following pages: **A fishing black bear searches the water for spawning salmon. Fish are the main source of winter fat for coastal bears.**

The Nimpkish researchers, who are now drafting recommendations concerning the logging of coastal black-bear habitat, say attention should be given to the preservation of good den sites. Trees with above-ground entrances are particularly important, as well as groves of escape trees for mothers and cubs.

While scientists recommend ways for black bears and loggers to use the same habitats, conservationists press for a ban on killing bears for sport. Each year, hunters legally shoot nearly 4,000 black bears in British Columbia. An Angus Reid poll commissioned by a group called Bear Watch proclaims that 91 percent of British Columbians are opposed to killing bears for their heads and hides. Bear Watch's call for a ban on trophy hunting has the backing of the Western Canada Wilderness Committee. Armed with a *Bear Protection Act* drafted by the Sierra Legal Defence Fund, WCWC has been soliciting support for a province-wide referendum on bear hunting.

Black bears inhabit most parts of the province, but no one is sure how many there are. Numbers from various sources range between 63,000 and 160,000. That much uncertainty emphasizes the special need for caution when deciding their fate in British Columbia.

opposite: **Coastal bears that feed on British Columbia salmon are among the province's largest, reaching as much as 300 kilograms before winter hibernation.**

following pages: **Clear river water drips from the snout of a fishing black bear as it bobs for salmon.**

BLACK BEAR
Ursus americanus

AVERAGE LENGTH:
1.3 to 1.9 metres.

AVERAGE WEIGHT:
Male, 60 to 300 kilograms; female, 40 to 80 kilograms.

LONGEVITY:
20 to 25 years in the wild.

BREEDING AGE:
Male, 4 to 5 years; female 3 to 4 years.

LITTER SIZE:
1 to 5, commonly 2.

DIET:
Roots, grasses, nuts, berries; insects, rodents, fawns, calves, salmon, occasionally other black bears.

PREDATORS:
Grizzlies, black bears, wolves, cougars, humans.

AVERAGE ANNUAL KILLS AND RELOCATIONS:
Hunters, 3,900; conservation officers, 800; relocations, 285.

ATTACKS ON HUMANS IN BRITISH COLUMBIA (1978 TO 1995):
9 killed; 79 injured.

CHARACTERISTICS:
Most plentiful of the world's bear species; mainly a forest animal, found in most of British Columbia.

STATUS IN BRITISH COLUMBIA:
A yellow-listed "Species Not at Risk"; population estimates, 63,000 to 160,000.